PRETEND YOU'RE IN TOKYO

東京にいる気分に

Michelle Mackintosh

Harper *by* Design

WELCOME
ようこそ

Yōkoso (welcome) to Tokyo. Japan's capital is one of the most eclectic and fascinating cities in the world. A trip to Tokyo will widen your perspective, change the way you see the world and maybe even make you a more receptive person in the process. I have been taking multiple trips to Tokyo each year of my adult life. Every time I get home, I try to bring back with me the city's magic to steel me for life's unpredictability. When work and everyday responsibilities start to feel overwhelming, I draw on my Tokyo life lessons and find I am ready to tackle almost anything.

Like most other large cities in Japan, Tokyo is a place defined by contrasts, with traditional gardens and temples set against neon jungles and looming skyscrapers. Narrow, lantern-filled alleyways branch off from vast and crowded boulevards, providing pockets of calm and spontaneous beauty. A perfect day in Tokyo might involve you floating into an elegant tearoom or stumbling into a messy drinking den. Whichever ways you like to explore in unfamiliar places, the immersive power of this city is sure to leave a lasting impression upon you long after your holiday is over.

Every time I fly to Tokyo, my heart is racing by the time I land at Haneda Airport. I feel the familiar excitement for *shokupan* (Japanese milk bread), gallery exhibitions, spectacular architecture and Tokyoites' innate sense of style. I've adopted so many Japanese-isms in my daily life, I can barely remember what life was like before my first visit. I have a deeper respect for nature's seasons, counting the days until my cherry blossom tree flowers or my maples turn crimson. I collect moss and make tiny displays inside my home. I whip up Japanese breakfasts on weekends and host picnics with homemade *bento* (lunch boxes). I read Japanese fiction and haiku poetry, write Tokyo-inspired snail mail to loved ones and drink a lot of green tea with friends.

Even if you're not a hardcore *shinnichi* (Japanophile) like myself, pretending you're in Tokyo can enrich your everyday life. This might be as simple as wandering your local streets and seeking beauty in unexpected places. You may spend an afternoon on the couch with pour-over coffee, bingeing YouTube clips from Tokyo train rides or tutorials on learning origami. Maybe pretending you're in Tokyo is sharing new food and drinks with friends, or just simply being inquisitive, open-minded and resourceful. Whether you're a seasoned traveller or dreaming of your first trip to Japan, I hope that this little book with take you on a journey to Tokyo from the comfort of your own home.

自然

NATURE

MOSS GARDEN

I love to visit Tokyo's gardens and temples in *tsuyu* (rainy season). They offer an escape from the big city, where you can disappear into the peacefulness of nature. I embark on any rainy day prepped with the essentials: a jacket, waterproof shoes and a cute umbrella. My focus is always drawn to the moss that knits a green carpet along pathways, makes its home underneath trees and slowly creeps over rocks. Rain makes the light more compelling and greens even greener, and the city's moss magically comes to life. Once moss makes itself known to you, its delicate beauty will always remind you of wistful days strolling in the Tokyo rain.

DIY When making a miniature moss garden, imagine a tiny version of yourself walking through its greenery. I like to make a hill and add a large rock and pebbles. You can even add your own *torii* gate (found at the entrance of a Shinto shrine) or *takuni* (racoon dog). Collect moss with an up-cycled plastic container and a small trowel. Walk the streets of your town looking for moss under trees, along the pavement or near drains and waterways. Make sure not to leave a mess or upset neighbours, and forage as many different varieties as possible. Choose a wide terracotta pot and fill it with soil, creating a rolling landscape. Arrange your mosses atop the soil, then add rocks and stones by following your artistic instincts. Give your new garden a daily spritz and weekly soak.

I fell in love with ikebana displays in the neighbourhood tea houses of Tokyo. Nothing is better than admiring the sparse beauty of Japanese floral displays while sitting on tatami mats and enjoying an afternoon matcha. Ikebana or *kadō* (way of flowers) is a refined art, with approaches varying from classical to strikingly modern. Seasonal foliage is often a guiding principle and the shaping of leaves is key. A flower might be the smallest part of a final scene or a few stems may be the hero. Ikebana can be simply described as 'the viewing of plants' which, to me, conveys its holistic and meditative approach. These are more than just pretty flowers, after all.

DIY Use an ikebana vase or shallow vessel as your canvas. Purists should seek out the proper ikebana tools: a *kenzan* (metal pronged base) and a pair of sharp scissors. These are needed to cut your greenery cleanly. Arrange each piece to stand tall (or weep sideways). Place your *kenzan* inside your vase or vessel. Collect branches, leaves and stems in three different lengths. Forage for intriguing twigs and flowers in your neighbourhood or buy some of your favourite seasonal blooms. Keep an eye out for branches with an unusual bend or distinctive shape, as these will help you create an eye-catching display. Check online to find an ikebana technique you like and start arranging and placing. Work thoughtfully and when you feel an emotional response to your arrangement, it's ready.

IKEBANA 生け花

MINI DRY GARDEN 枯山水

My favourite dry garden in Tokyo lives on the roof of International House, a mid-century members' club in Roppongi. *Karesansui* (landscaped rock gardens) are contemplation spaces dating back to the birth of Zen Buddhism in Japan in the 1300s. Mimicking space and time – or oceans and islands – these artfully placed rocks and raked stones form patterns that are a form of meditation. When life gets busy at home, it's important to take time out to relax your mind. I like to place a small dry garden on my desk, right next to my computer, and remind myself to take one breath at a time.

DIY Making a small-scale *karesansui* at home couldn't be simpler. You'll need fine stones or sand to fill a shallow rectangular container – I use a bamboo or wooden box lid. Forage some interesting rocks and place them on your sandy base. Odd numbers are always more interesting; I usually settle on three. If you're finding it hard to source rocks, try aquarium stores (they also sell driftwood, which could be a welcome addition to your dry garden). Tiny wooden rakes are available online, but you can also use a bamboo fork. Introduce Zen stacking stones (again, in odd numbers) to lend your dry garden some gravitas. Just make sure you place your dry garden away from your cat, who will nudge your stones onto the ground (and might mistake your creation for kitty litter).

You can't help but be aware of the seasons while in Tokyo. They dictate what I pack for my visits. Rainy season? Raincoat. High summer? Ultra-light linen and cotton. To complement the blossoms or autumn leaves? Pink and ochre dresses. I relish walking through Tokyo and sensing the change when the city farewells one micro season and welcomes the next. These shifts are entrenched in Japanese culture, as the ancient calendar is broken down into 24 *sekki* (seasons) and 72 micro seasons which last roughly five *kō* (days). Seasonal names are pure poetry, like *Insects Awaken, Caterpillars Become Butterflies, Frogs Start Singing, Worms Surface* or *Bamboo Shoots Sprout.*

DIY Dedicate a small notebook to a five-day micro season of your own making. Carefully observe your natural surroundings and write down the things you see and hear. This will help you name your micro season and tell its story. Sit in local green spaces or travel to a special garden. Look for flowers blooming, leaves falling, dewdrops on plant life and the crisp chill of morning. Listen to the sound of birds and insects. Breathe in the air deeply. I always take a little container to pick up leaves or seedpods discarded by the trees. With washi or painter's tape, press leaves and flowers into your notebook, writing words and observations around them. You could turn these musings into poems or haiku. This is a great activity to do with friends or little ones.

MICRO
SEASONS

七十二候

YORISHIRO TREES 依り代

While Meiji Jingu – a vast Shinto shrine – is one of Tokyo's biggest tourist attractions, it can still feel like a very private experience. It's almost as if the shrine exists for you alone to contemplate and walk around. Shinto, Japan's oldest religion, holds the belief that *kami* (spirits, deities or gods) can inhabit *yorishiro* (nature and objects). These *yorishiro* are distinguished by a *shimenawa* (sacred prayer rope) looped around their mid-section. At Meiji Jingu, two colossal *yorishiro* trees at the shrine are intrinsically linked by *shimenawa*. In their presence, we can feel the deep spiritual connection to nature that's celebrated in Japan.

DIY This is the perfect project for a favourite tree in your garden. Or you could make this a group project to temporarily decorate trees in the park for a picnic. *Shimenawa* is made by plaiting hemp, jute or heavy twine. Check online for an authentic technique or simply plait long pieces of twine and wrap them around your tree. If you're feeling adventurous, add zig-zagged and folded *shide* (white paper) between rope loops and tassels. Now you're ready to sit under your own *yorishiro* tree when meditating at home. If you're curious to find out more, the *Kojiki* and *Nihon Shoki* are Japan's oldest texts that chronicle its spiritual history and creation mythology.

POTTED STREET GARDEN
鉢植えのストリートガーデン

In neighbourhood Tokyo, you'll find moments of nature in unexpected places. Back streets are bursting with greenery and small potted gardens line residential streets. Hopping off the Tōkyū Tōyoko Line train, I love to wander past the jumble of pots that bloom with peculiar plants. Bonsai, *kokedama* (moss balls), sweet-smelling flowers and tiny autumn trees are always on display. I love watching locals tend their mini forests, carefully watering each plant with love and care. Tokyo's quirky solutions to high-density living show that no matter where you live and how small your garden is, there are endless ways to get creative with nature.

DIY If you live in an apartment or small house, you can still practice the floral arts in your own potted garden. Perfect for renters and share houses, potted plants are easy to move and collect. If you live directly on the street, you can start a potted jungle at your front door. I have a verandah replete with pots, rocks and stones, hanging dried natives and *kokedama*. Make sure to ask your local nursery what grows best in pots and tell them what kind of natural light you have available. If you have any green-thumbed friends, ask them for cuttings to propagate. Even try sprouting an avocado tree from the stone of the fruit. Potted street gardens lead to great conversations with neighbours that you might not yet have had the chance to meet.

JAPANESE PLANTS & FLOWERS

日本の植物や花

Each season, Tokyo proudly shows its colours. Maples in autumn and cherry blossoms in spring. Summer lotus with their giant seedpods and plum blossoms that signal the end of winter. In Kamakura, Meigetsu-in is known as the hydrangea temple. Its gardens swell with the striking, rounded flower that remains in bloom all year round. To climb the temple stairs and be engulfed by this floral ocean is to experience a moment of pure Japanese serenity. The iconic ginkgo leaf is the official symbol of Tokyo. When I witnessed rows of the dazzling golden trees on Icho Namiki Dori (or Ginkgo Avenue) in the height of autumn, I understood why.

DIY In my hometown, I stumbled across a street with ginkgo trees by complete chance. Now, I return every year with a thermos of green tea to admire the sight of glittering golden leaves. In Japan, this autumnal pilgrimage is called *momijigari* (red leaf hunting, or what some North Americans call 'leaf peeping'). Hop online and see if there's a garden with Japanese plant-life near you. If any leaves or flowers have fallen from their homes, collect them from the garden floor. Press these souvenirs inside the pages of your favourite books to rediscover them the next time you read the book. I like to sandwich pressed leaves and flowers in picture frames to display them around my house.

Tsubo-niwa (courtyard gardens) have been built into Japanese homes for hundreds of years. These compact spaces are often framed entirely by windows, giving residents of small abodes the chance to tend to and admire nature in a restorative way. Features of a *tsubo-niwa* are a *chōzubachi* (stone basin), rocks varying in size from stepping stones to feature boulders, moss and a deciduous tree like a Japanese maple. With a *tsubo-niwa*, anyone can experience the changing of leaves and enjoy micro seasons from the comfort of their own home. You don't need a sprawling backyard to tap into the natural world.

DIY Make your own *tsubo-niwa* in a small outdoor space, courtyard, balcony, verandah or even inside your home. Make a garden mood board for inspiration, using either Pinterest or a paper collage, and decide on all your favourite elements. Remember: don't make things too complicated. A pocket-sized garden is all about simplicity and a few stylistic choices. Choose a tree that always catches your eye – I love maple, ginkgo, mini yuzu or persimmon. Visit a local landscaping store or nursery and explain to them the available natural light in the space you've set aside for a *tsubo-niwa*. Moss can be sourced from your neighbourhood's drains. Grasses and pebbles are also easily foraged and would make perfect additions to your compact garden. *Tsubo-niwa* can house a little stone lantern or shrine, too – if you're so inclined.

TSUBO-NIWA 坪庭

BONSAI 盆栽

The art of the bonsai (which translates to 'tray planting') is well known in the West. One of Japan's most iconic cultural exports, bonsai is a meditation on patience, nature and beauty. Bonsai trees are planted in shallow trays, then cut, pruned and manicured, creating the appearance of a mature tree that's shrunk down to something you can hold in one hand. Bonsai have a poetic, mesmerising quality when they're shaped to look twisted and windswept. I love to visit the Omiya Bonsai Village, which is just outside Tokyo in Saitama. If you arrive in autumn or the blossom season, you'll experience the magical changing of leaves on a tiny scale.

DIY Bonsai can be costly, but they're also fun and easy to grow at home. Do some online research to find a tree you love that's also good for a bonsai novice. Pine, juniper or cyprus are my favourites. Buy a tray or shallow pot and some bonsai soil so your plant has the right balance of nutrients. Lift your mini tree out of its container and trim the root ball so it fits in your pot. Carefully arrange the tree and roots into a position you think looks best, then gently pack the roots with soil to secure in place. Using good-quality scissors or bonsai tools, pare back the branches until your tree takes on a strong, graphic shape. Be patient and train your tree over time.

Space is a luxury in Tokyo, so the likelihood of owning a sizable garden of your own is remote for most residents and businesses. Luckily, a *chōzubachi* (stone basin) can be placed anywhere. Water features don't require natural light – or even much room – to survive and create ambience. I've seen them in bathrooms, at front doors, next to lanterns and beside kneeling stones. They are full of still water and decorated with pebbles and floating leaves. *Chōzubachi* might be accompanied by a *shishi-odoshi* (deer scarer) or bamboo tap flowing with water and make a perfect addition to a *tsubo-niwa* (courtyard garden).

DIY *Chōzubachi* are a simple way to bring stillness and the calming effect of water into your everyday life. Plus, they're incredibly versatile for landscaping. Look up a supplier in your area and see what they have in stock. If you've got plenty of old unused pots at home, just repurpose a round one with a rustic look and plug the drainage hole in the bottom. If it's terracotta, buy a small tin of concrete paint and apply a few coats to the outside of the pot to create the illusion of greying stone. Add some dark, flat pebbles to the bottom of your pot and fill with water. Float three foraged flowers or leaves on top. Placement is key, so consider carefully where you would most enjoy your *chōzubachi*.

手水鉢

CHŌZUBACHI

HANAMI

花見

Seeing Tokyo in *hanami* (cherry blossom season) will change your life. The first time I saw the city sparkling with blossoms, the air was crisp and the mood was electrifying. Rows or clusters of *sakura* (cherry blossom) trees filled my favourite gardens, like Inokashira Park, Shinjuku Gyoen and Ueno Koen. The path along the Nakameguro canal was decorated with lanterns and countless rows of blossom trees bursting with life. *Hanami* – also used to describe the 'flower viewing' – takes place in late March and early April. Walking around the city at this time of year is a joyous experience as *hanami* brings together all walks of life. Groups of friends and families celebrate under every blossoming tree. The elderly and frail are joined by their pets and loved ones while everyone enjoys food (and maybe a cheeky sake) beneath the new flowers.

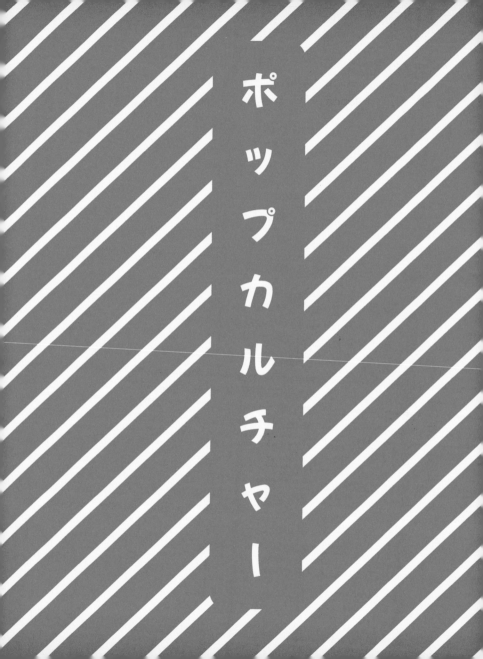

ポップカルチャー

POP

—

CULTURE

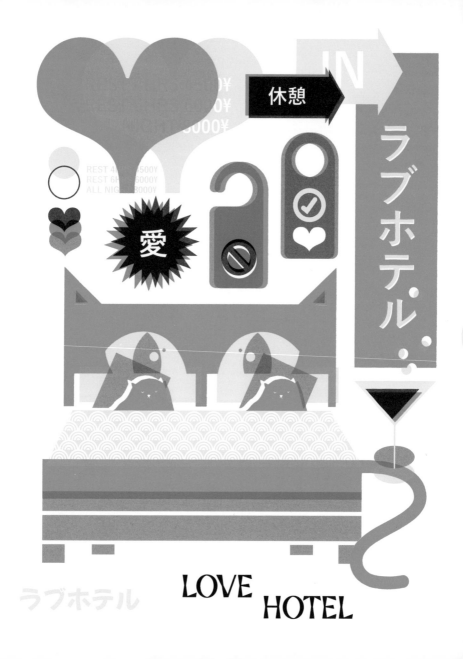

Tokyo's mysterious Love Hotels started popping up in the late 1960s to accommodate couples on secret rendezvous. Their eye-popping exteriors are emblazoned with an assortment of English and Japanese in gaudy neon signage. Located in clusters around hip areas like Shinjuku or Shibuya, Love Hotel prices are low and customer expectations are high. Each hotel usually has a quirky, completely over-the-top theme. Visiting couples pay by the hour for their short stay, whether it's a 'nooner' or just some classic afternoon delight.

DIY To recreate the romantic escapism of a Love Hotel at home, pick a theme and really stick to it. If your partner is game, get busy constructing a fantasy with gender-neutral geisha, naughty ninjas, sexy samurais, J-POP star lookalikes or kimono-clad beauties. Whatever flavours your miso, make sure you deeply commit to your concept with cocktails, snacks, music and decor. From a blanket fort in the lounge room to moon viewing in your garden, think outside the box and go wild with costumes, cardboard cutouts and signage. Just don't be surprised if, on your next trip to Tokyo, you find yourself particularly enamoured with billboards for Hello Kitty or Pokémon.

POP CULTURE

Tokyo's *neko* (cat) cafes are the purr-fect hang-out for local animal lovers, cute couples on dates and *gaijin* (Westerners) who are heartsick for their fur babies back home. Whenever I pass a *kawaii* (cute) cat-centric sign in Tokyo, I ditch any other plans and spend an hour meeting and relaxing with new feline friends. Entering any *neko* cafe is a delicate dance – patting a few kitties (if they let me) while drinking tea in a cat-themed cup and admiring the lively decor. To relish the symphony of purrs and watch a clowder of cats manoeuvre over occupied tables and chairs is the ultimate kind of therapy.

DIY To establish your cat cafe, prep some biscuits and cakes in advance. You can buy some cat-shaped biscuit cutters, but adding ears and whiskers to various snacks – or yourself – is just as effective. Fill your cafe with soft furnishings and plush toys (Hello Kitty-themed is a bonus), and make a relevant playlist featuring Cat Stevens, Cat Power, 'The Love Cats' by The Cure, 'Cat Claw' by The Kills and 'I am a Cat' by Shonen Knife. I like to do a Cheshire Cat reading and stream clips of kittens to really set the scene. Your furry companion can help (or hinder) this set-up by providing art direction on cushion placement, blanket folding and cosy space selection. Dog, bunny and guinea pig owners need not despair – this concept is transferable to any pet cafe of your choosing.

FASHION ファッション

Tokyo designers are famous for putting a distinct twist on basics, streetwear and high fashion. Each trip I take to Tokyo has the same itinerary for day one: I walk a full circle of Shibuya, Omotesando and Harajuku, scouring the best shops and scoping out how Tokyoites create their ensembles. I'm always compelled by the colours, lengths, layering and quirks. I may be drawn to a septuagenarian with striking glasses, a salaryman with glaringly bright sneakers or a stylish couple with asymmetrical haircuts. Unsurprisingly, after so many visits my favourite wardrobe basics have acquired a Tokyo twist.

DIY Use the motivation of an upcoming event, date night or entire season by trying out an adventurous new look at home. Start a mood board to hone your colour palette and style vibe. Raid your wardrobe's back catalogue or hunt through thrift shops to find anything and everything that works with your vision. Start slowly by adding an element or two, building up to hero looks for parties and events. Your Tokyo-inspired style may present itself subtly, like adding bright socks when you would have otherwise gone for black. You might put neon laces on your sneakers. Or perhaps you'll end up with a complete wardrobe revamp. Your research skills and colour knowledge will go beyond the clothes you wear and start to permeate the overall style of your home, your accessories and possibly even the outfits you choose for your pet.

Tokyo is one of the best places in the world for a big night out. When beer and sake starts flowing, it's more than likely you'll end up at a karaoke venue. The most popular karaoke (meaning 'empty orchestra') goes down in themed parlours that charge by the hour, with outrageous styling and enough drinks to turn even the most reluctant vocalist or mild-mannered colleague into a bona fide diva. Room themes vary according to budget, but some include cult films, gaudy futurism and (of course) robots. Whatever your choice of music or decor, karaoke is the quintessential Tokyo night out.

DIY To host a karaoke night you'll need a device, sound mixer, microphone, TV or monitor screen, good internet for YouTube and a decent speaker. You may want to warn your neighbours in advance. Get a tech-savvy friend to spearhead the setup or just hire a karaoke machine for the evening. Prepare some social lubricant in the form of crazy cocktails, highballs and giant jugs of beer to help everyone get into the mood. Rockstar diva, pop icon or indie-folk princess – pick your poison (or go full Poison with a heavy metal theme). Dress to impress and don't forget to make some memorable decorations, like cardboard cutout guitars, and some snacks so none of your guests are drinking on empty stomachs.

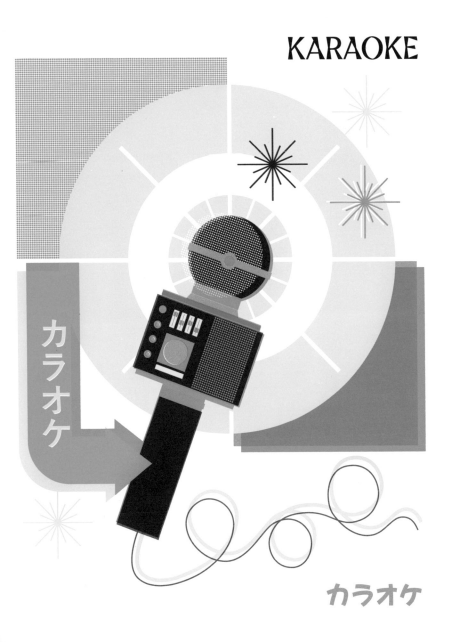

KARAOKE

カラオケ

カラオケ

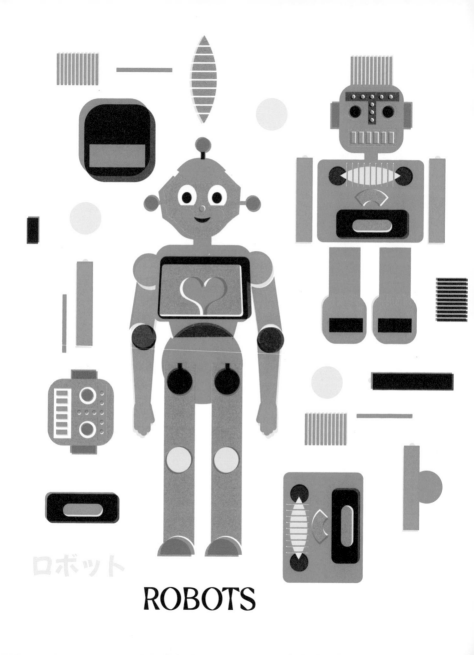

ロボット

ROBOTS

Do you prefer humanoids to humans? Head straight to Akihabara in Tokyo where you can geek out over robot collectables and fun vintage buys. To see Tokyo's robo-obsession come (quite literally) to life, visit the Statue of Unicorn Gundam in Diver City. My favourite robot experience is the permanent exhibition at Miraikan (National Museum of Emerging Science and Innovation) which gives you a peek into Japan's cutting-edge Artificial Intelligence technologies. Old-school robots, like the beloved protagonist of *Gigantor*, seemed like a futuristic dream just a few decades ago, but robots are now commonplace in Tokyo. Robotic and digital customer service interfaces can be found in many restaurants, hotels and shops.

DIY You can turn your willing child or amenable pet into a robot by drawing or painting mechanoid features on a cardboard box. Use a smaller box for the head and place it atop a larger one for the body. Glue or tape the two pieces together. Add flexible duct tubing for arms to create your own classic robot costume. Spend an afternoon watching classic Tokyo robot films or TV shows like *The Mysterians* (1957), *Astroboy* (1963), *Godzilla vs. Megalon* (1973) and *Tetsuo: The Iron Man* (1989), along with Japanese snacks and a *bīru* (beer) or two.

MANGA 漫画

The kanji characters for the word manga translate simply as 'man and pictures'. This has always struck me as the perfect way to describe the thriving culture of graphic novels and illustrated books. The manga market has something for everyone, with themes from erotica to the supernatural, schoolyard antics and domestic life. Everywhere you go in Tokyo, people are reading manga – from salarymen on public transport to a young mum in a cafe. I look for vintage examples of manga with their strong graphic styling and bold colours, and recently bought some children's manga to help my Japanese language studies.

DIY Ask your local library if they stock Japanese graphic novels or scope out second-hand copies online. Some bigger cities outside of Japan have specialty retailers that stock manga titles. Find out what's popular in your favourite genres and ask your friends and group chats to see if anyone has copies they can lend you. If you're artistically minded, why not make your own manga? Research their structure (reading right to left, top to bottom) and character archetypes, then start inventing some stories of your own. You'll probably need your story to feature a hero, villain, creepy side-character and otherworldly elements and oddities. Keep your colour palette limited and don't be afraid to let your manga wander into moments of melancholy – the literary possibilities of the form are limitless.

キャラクター

CHARACTERS

Giant fluffy animals, hybrid creatures and inanimate objects pop out from street corners, dance on screens and sing on the back of trucks all over Tokyo. Every brand in Japan seems to have a mascot. It might feel nonsensical, but these characters are sure to put an instant smile on your face and remind you that you're passing through a culture vastly different from your own. Devotees of *Pokémon*, *My Neighbor Totoro*, *Doraemon* and *Hello Kitty* can purchase collectables from stores dedicated specifically to these beloved characters. Be prepared to return from Tokyo with a suitcase filled with character-based toys, fluffy keyrings, stationery, t-shirts, socks and more.

DIY Spend an afternoon designing a character of your own. Firstly, give them a name and write down some personality traits. Decide on a colour palette, body shape and facial features, then get drawing. This is a great group project, especially if you set a time limit. When time is up, everyone can do a show and tell alongside some music they think matches their creation. Finally, when your character is fully formed, think about making cupcakes and decorating them with your new friend's face. You can even use your designs to personalise birthday invites or holiday cards.

Japanese Pop (or J-POP) has broken through to Western audiences with hit girl-groups, viral dance moves and iconic costumes. J-POP stars like Kyary Pamyu Pamyu – with her neon styling, vibrant video clips and cute lyrics – have burst out of the Tokyo bubble, while others such as BABYMETAL have a cult following for their darker and hybridised brands of pop. AKB48 have an enormous local fanbase, performing every day at their home stage in Akihabara and constantly adding and swapping out members. If you're intrigued, Tokyo's largest music stores like Tower Records or Disc Union have entire floors dedicated to homegrown pop.

DIY

DIY Ask your smart home device or reluctant housemate to fire up a J-POP anthem playlist. Then organise a J-POP party at yours (or, if you're like me, a J-indies party). Send out a physical invite for friends to dress *kawaii* (cute) and to brainstorm their own music requests. Go old-school and request Shonen Knife or Pizzicato Five, the futurist pop of Perfume (check out their matching outfits for some excellent inspiration), dance around the house to indie pop darlings Homecomings or unapologetically demand the newcomer boyband INI. School uniforms, pastel wigs, frills and tartan make for great J-POP costumes. Design a fabulous solo outfit, or form a girl group or boy band (regardless of your collective genders). For an extra-special touch, trawl through YouTube for the best J-POP dance moves and break them out after a few drinks.

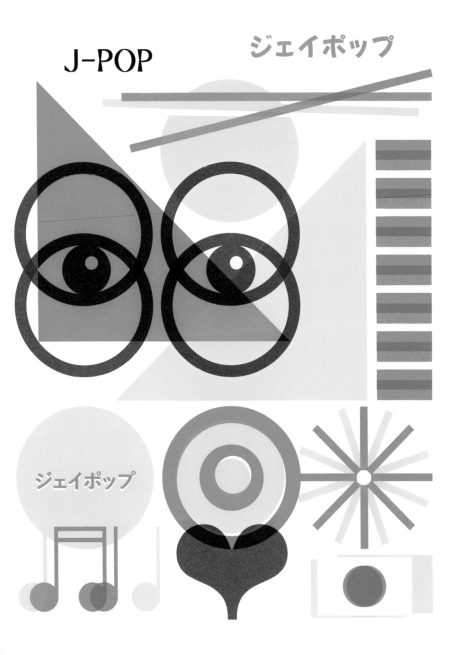

J-POP

ジェイポップ

ジェイポップ

VENDING MACHINES
自動販売機

You'll find vending machines peddling all manner of wares across Tokyo, sometimes in the most unexpected places. Gaining popularity in the 1950s, and taking off in the 1960s in time for the Tokyo Olympics, these thirst- or hunger-quenching machines have become part of the city's landscape. Most serve up hot and cold drinks, but you can also find those dispensing booze, soups, fruit and vegetables, toys, shirts, ties, underwear, condoms and feminine products. Thankfully, most vending machines have inbuilt recycling bins, so after you've downed a refreshing Pocari Sweat or can of energising Boss coffee, you can be confident that it won't end up as landfill.

DIY Unless you're willing to spend thousands of dollars on a real unit, the only way to have your own vending machine at home is by drawing one onto a cardboard box. Create drink names from scratch. See if you can find some classic Japanese brands at your local supermarket or Asian grocer. Make sure each item has a corresponding number below it. Visitors can say: 'I'll have A1 please' or 'Just a Calpis Water, thanks'. Include a button grid on the right-hand side of your box and a push flap at the bottom. If you have kids or young relatives, enlist them to do the sound effects of your cardboard vending machine's whirring and clunking.

自動販売機

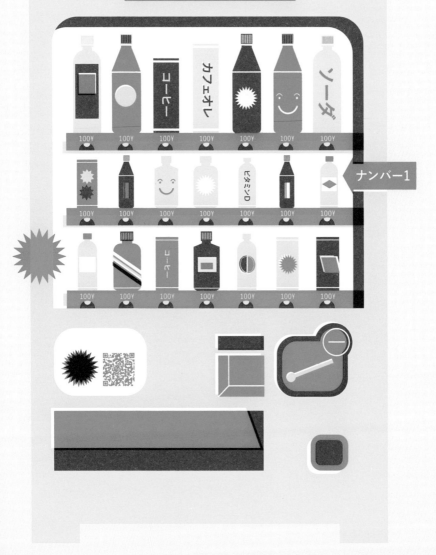

Tokyo is the home of pop culture collectables. At specialty stores, queues form around the block, sometimes days in advance, for limited-edition vinyl, toys, trainers, skateboards and all things fashion. You can find anything from a Murakami sunflower cushion to a BE@RBRICK (mini bear figurine) with the Eames Office print and an amazing array of limited edition *gashapon* (capsule toys). This culture of rare collectables creates jobs for up-and-coming designers, who make sure the products never become stale. They're sustainable, too. If you have no more use for a collectable, you can sell it second-hand for a good price or donate it to a charity where you know it will find a loving home.

DIY
Why not start your own mini-collection of something close to your heart? I collect international stamps from pen friends' letters and scour op shops for vintage additions to my ever-growing button collection. You could collect leaves and press them in a special book, antique sewing patterns, matchboxes or even verbal family stories from older relatives and write them down. Whatever it is you decide to collect make sure you have something lovely to use as storage for your collection. This could be an old jewellery box or heirloom suitcase, or if you want to display your collection use it to fill a large glass vase.

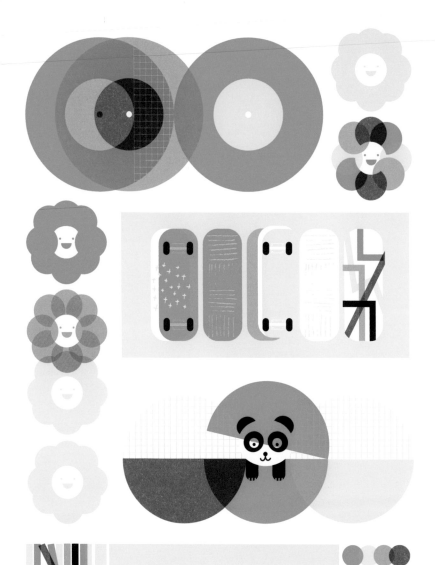

COLLECTABLES 収集品

YAMANOTE LOOP

山手線

In wintertime, when temperatures hover around zero, I like to ride Tokyo's Yamanote train loop around the city and hop off at stations I've never visited before that look interesting through the window. The secret charm of this train is the heating beneath the seats (and some even have TV screens blaring colourful, jingle-heavy advertising). There are 30 stations on the loop including popular destinations like Harajuku, Shibuya and Shinjuku. However, it also bisects some of my favourite smaller neighbourhoods like Ebisu (home of jeans and beer) and Meguro, which is a short walk from Nakameguro, where weeping cherry blossoms line the canal in late March or April.

飲
食

FOOD
&
DRINK

KONBINI TAMAGO SANDO

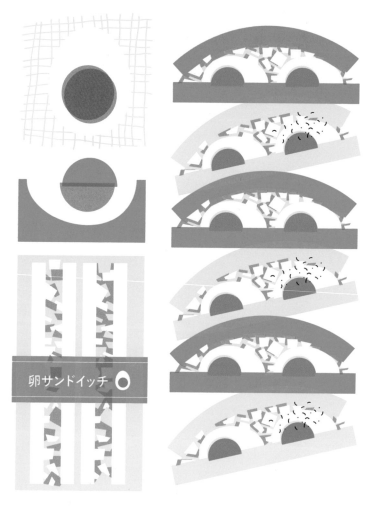

卵サンドイッチ

コンビニ　卵サンド

Whether you find it a delicious snack or secret shame, this fluffy white bread *tamago sando* (egg sandwich) is a staple of Tokyo's *konbini* (convenience stores). Lawson, FamilyMart, Sunkus and smaller franchises each have their own take on the perennial favourite, enhancing the filling with kewpie mayonnaise or any number of mystery ingredients. It's the kind of snack that creeps up on you – just walking past a convenience store can bring about that deep yearning. A classic example of *yōshoku* (Western food with a Japanese twist), the iconic egg sandwich is a must-have in Tokyo and an *oishii* (delicious) treat to make at home.

DIY Tokyo-style *tamago sando* is a great grab-and-go snack for *bento* (lunch boxes), picnics or alfresco dining. Make sure you have fluffy white bread similar to *shokupan* (Japanese milk bread), free-range eggs and high-quality butter. The quality of your ingredients will make or break your *sando*. Check online for clever recipes and take the Goldilocks approach (taste and re-taste your sandwich creations) until you find your favourite. Stack egg and bread in layers to contrast the golden yellow with bright white. I like making a special version with a whole boiled egg in the centre, so when the *sando* is cut in half it reveals the image of an incredible floating egg.

Many of Tokyo's historic gardens – like Hamarikyu, Shinjuku Gyoen, Rikugien and Kiyosumi – have their own teahouse where I love to let the afternoon pass by while drinking matcha and admiring the view. Always served in a *chawan* (flat-bottomed ceramic bowl), matcha is made by whisking powdered green tea in hot water to create the perfect amount of frothiness. The kettle used, water temperature and the *chawan* are all part of this ritual, which has roots in Zen Buddhism. Westerners are taking up matcha as a daily health drink thanks to its high antioxidant levels, but in Japan, the beloved flavour is found in everything from soft-serve ice cream to KitKats.

DIY Take a trip to your local Japanese or Asian grocer and buy a small tin of matcha powder. A *chawan*, *chasen* (bamboo whisk) and *chashaku* (tea scoop) can be found at Japanese homewares stores or online. Pour a little hot water into your matcha bowl and start to combine with your whisk by flicking your wrist in W-shaped motions, back and forth. When combined, add the rest of your hot water and repeat the back and forth movements until your matcha starts to froth. Briskly whisk the top of your tea to create that iconic bubbling foam. Many Japanese cafes serve a wonderful bowl of matcha, so next time you're out and about, try substituting your coffee or English breakfast for a bowl of matcha.

抹茶

MATCHA

KISSATEN 喫茶店

Coffee culture in Tokyo can be traced back to the Meiji Era (1868–1912) and has a completely different feel to the espresso-dominated scene of the West. A little bit Viennese, with a dash of French and a splash of Americana, *kissaten* (tearooms and coffee shops) are distinctly Japanese. With retro signage, mood lighting and dark interiors, these atmospheric cafes pride themselves on serving pour-over coffee (black or with cream) and a sweet treat, like chiffon cake. *Kissaten* are often owned by couples and can be as quiet and peaceful as a library, even when every table is full. The kanji for *kissaten* translate as drink, eat and smoke – perfectly describing the hazy heydays of the cool Tokyo retro cafe.

DIY Setting up a home *kissaten* is a great idea if you are hosting a book club or a small birthday soiree for a friend. *Kissaten* are the place for reading and ideas, quiet places to drink and deep whispered conversation. You'll need a pour-over gooseneck kettle, paper filters, filter holder, glass jug (I love Kalita, but Kinto is a great brand, too) and coffee beans ground to the pour-over setting. Fill your *kissaten* with books and magazines, set some mood lighting and include the perfect pour-over companion: the chiffon cake (I make a maple syrup version which you can find online). Don't forget to put on a soundtrack of slinky jazz. You'll need all the coffee accoutrements (milk, cream and sugar) and seriously good-quality beans. If you don't have the equipment for pour-over, stovetop espresso would suffice (although your *kissaten's* authenticity is at stake).

Getting lost in Tokyo Station is a rite of passage for any Western traveller. My first experience was filled with disorienting thoughts: 'Oh no, where's my exit?', 'Ooooh, look at her blue outfit and matching bag' and 'Hang on, what is that bright yellow sign of a banana wearing a bow?' Yes, the gargantuan station was the first time I came across the city's greatest unofficial souvenir, the Tokyo Banana. The delicious, sweet treat is a fluffy sponge wrapped around a banana cream filling. Perfect to take home in your bag (they last around five days in my extensive experience) or for a pitstop on your day tramping around the capital.

DIY If you're feeling heartsick for Tokyo, making your own Tokyo Banana should be on your to-do list. Check online for great recipes or devise your own if you're an intuitive cook. If opting for the latter, the rolling process may prove to be a little tricky – just remember, your banana doesn't need to be flawless, it just has to transport you back to Tokyo. Try making your own packaging for your banana with a paper lunch bag tied up with washi tape. Invite fellow Tokyo-philes over for afternoon tea and surprise them with a nostalgic treat.

東京バナナ

TOKYO

BANANA

Outsiders may think of sushi or teriyaki chicken as being classically Tokyo, but locals and regular visitors are obsessed with *yōshoku* (Western food with a Japanese twist). The allure of *shokupan* (Japanese milk bread) should not be lost on you. Fluffy and blindingly white, *shokupan* is the fairy floss of bread. Its sweetness makes it both moreish and somewhat baffling to *gaijin* (Westerners), who might be accustomed to breads like wholewheat or sourdough. *Departo* (department store) food halls have many bakeries to try, but areas that surged in popularity immediately post-war, like Ginza, are home to establishments like Centre – which always has queues for its *shokupan* winding around the block.

DIY *Shokupan* cravings can often be easily satisfied, with local artisan bakers in Western cities experimenting with milk breads. There are also achievable recipes available online. I always make mine with the Yudane method (using equal parts flour and boiling water). When your bread is out of the oven and slightly cooled, cut it into slices no less then 3cm thick. The thicker the slice, the more impressive your meal becomes. I serve *shokupan* straight out of the oven with an array of accompanying spreads. For the most authentic topping, try boiling red beans with sugar to make *anko* (red bean paste). I then add a dollop next to a perfect square of butter on my 'biggu toasto' and enjoy with a pour-over coffee. *Shokupan* is best eaten while warm, so invite over your nearest and dearest for a perfect slice of Tokyo.

HOSHIGAKI 干し柿

One of my all-time favourite autumn foods in Tokyo is *hoshigaki* (dried persimmons). In the *wagashi* (Japanese sweets) section of the flagship Isetan department store in Shinjuku, I'm always happy to join the long queue and secure this seasonal treat. The air-dried fruit has an almost leathery exterior that gives way to a soft, caramelised centre. *Hoshigaki* have hints of honey and spice, and are a little bit sweet, quite sticky and inarguably delicious. Autumn in Tokyo would not be the same without *hoshigaki*.

DIY Collect underripe, astringent persimmons with the stems still attached. You'll need some cotton twine and a peeler. Peel persimmons carefully then spray with *shōchū* (Japanese spirit) or vodka to sterilise. Knot twine around each stem and hang outside under the eaves or verandah your home, to protect them from the weather. After seven days, start to massage the persimmons by hand. This helps break down sugars. After around four or six weeks, your dried fruit will be ready to eat. Your *hoshigaki* will change colour and texture along the way. The white surface that appears on your fruit is not any kind of mould, but simply edible sugars.

TINY TOKYO BAR　　東京の小さなバー

Tokyo is known for its tiny bars, which are often standing room only or seating for six people (or less). These bars hide in plain sight: under bridges, down skinny alleyways and above nondescript shopfronts. The iconic *yokocho* (alleyways) around Shibuya, Shinjuku and Ueno stations are home to some of the city's smallest and most fascinating drinking holes. Drink like a local and order a highball, *shōchū* (Japanese spirit) or whisky sour. My tipples of choice are *shōchū* topped up with green tea, sake cocktails and *umeshu* (plum liquor) and soda. Salty bar snacks like wasabi peas or *kakipi* (tiny rice crackers and nuts) are perfect accompaniments. The more adventurous can try honeyed spanner crabs, fermented squid and fish jerky.

DIY Choose a small room or corner in your house to set up a bar counter. If you've got a flair for branding, you may want to name and brand the bar, designing a logo and stamping it onto coasters. Arrange different alcohol, mixers and different sized glasses along your bar ready for your limited and exclusive clientele (namely your partner, friends and cat). Find recipes online for an *umeshu* soda, lemon sour and soy milk sake cocktail.

With a reputation for having one of the healthiest breakfasts in world cuisine, the Japanese really know how to nourish your body for the day ahead. Variations of miso soup, rice, pickles and perhaps grilled fish or an omelette are all washed down with green tea. Train stations can be some of the best places to find a great Japanese breakfast and paying a little extra at a *ryokan* (traditional Japanese inn) is something you have to experience at least once in your visit to Tokyo. Fortifying and delicious, eating breakfast as the Japanese do might make you rethink the way you wake up at home.

DIY I like to make Japanese breakfast on weekends. That way I can make my miso broth from scratch in a leisurely fashion and arrange each element in carefully considered ceramics and vessels. I always buy good-quality Japanese rice, a small piece of fish, eggs for a rolled omelette, tofu for the miso and a cucumber to whip up some quick homemade pickles. Remember to always eat breakfast with chopsticks. If you don't have time to make your own Japanese breakfast, seek out a cafe in your neighbourhood that does Tokyo-style mornings authentically.

JAPANESE
BREAKFAST

朝ごはん

MATCHA CHIZUKEKI
抹茶チーズケーキ

Raw, sweet and sour all at once, my favourite treat for afternoon tea in Tokyo is matcha *chizukeki* (cheesecake). Light and delicious, its flavour and texture are unlike anything I've ever found in my recipe books at home. I always make time to visit my most treasured Shimokitazawa cafe, snuggle into one of their perfectly worn armchairs and while away a few hours. Most importantly, this involves matcha-flavoured cheesecake served with a dollop of red bean paste on the side, washed down with a *hojicha* (roasted green tea) latte or filtered coffee.

DIY Take your favourite raw cheesecake recipe and add sifted matcha powder to the cream cheese filling after the mixture is combined, giving it a zest of green tea. Try swapping out half of the cream with yoghurt for a lighter filling. I can never seem to find a recipe that matches my dreamy Tokyo cheesecake, so I've concocted my own. I make my filling with equal parts Greek yoghurt, mascarpone, cream cheese and melted white chocolate, sifting in the matcha powder at the end and tasting it until I have the right balance of sweetness and bitterness.

I was a little frightened of *oden* (a one-pot soup) the first few times I saw it at the *konbini* (convenience store). The bubbling soup of unidentifiable ingredients looked too exposed, confusing and potentially dangerous. It wasn't until friends ordered *oden* at an *izakaya* (casual bar) dinner that I understood the beauty and nuance of this slow-cooked Tokyo staple. Essentially a rustic stew, *oden* might contain egg, tofu, vegetables or seafood, but it's always slowly boiled in a delicious broth. It makes for a warming winter meal or an excellent side dish. It's a great pick-me-up if you're feeling under the weather: filling, but gentle on the stomach.

DIY Make one litre of dashi, or your own veggie, fish or chicken stock (you can also find *oden* broth at some select Asian grocers). Place stock in an earthenware pot with a lid. Add 5 tablespoons each of mirin, soy sauce (more if you love soy), cooking sake, a piece of kelp and a few tablespoons of sugar. Taste test and adjust then bring to the boil. Peel and slice daikon radish and small potatoes, then place in the broth to boil for 30 minutes. Then cook for an extra 10 minutes with boiled and peeled eggs, tofu puffs and carrot sliced into flower cuts. Turn the heat off, put the lid on and let steep for an hour. Warm up and serve in small bowls with spring onion and a little bit of mustard.

ODEN おでん

BENTO

弁当

Compact, colourful and clever, these compartmentalised meals are a Tokyo staple and one of my favourite reasons to visit. *Bento* (lunch boxes) are sustainable, reusable food containers for both Japanese school children and adults. Perfect for long train trips, picnics or really any situation, a bento will make you rethink how you eat your lunch.

伝
統

TRADITION

SEKIMORI ISHI 関守石

A *sekimori ishi* (boundary guard stone), also called *tomeishi*, is a rock knotted with twine in a very particular way. It is placed on a path and indicates that you should not walk any further, or more literally 'do not enter' or 'staff only'. Any area beyond a *sekimori ishi* is private. These are common in tea and zen gardens, but I've also seen them in small gardens in restaurants and cafes. On one of my first trips to Tokyo, I was exploring the immersive garden at the Nezu Museum when I came across a midsize rock wrapped in twine. As I contemplated its meaning, a museum volunteer appeared and kindly explained the significance of a *sekimori ishi*, which just made perfect and beautiful sense to me.

DIY A *sekimori ishi* can have meaning in your home in a variety of ways. All you need is need a midsize rock and thick twine or rope to make your own. From experience, I can tell you that it may take a bit of time until the perfect rock presents itself. Research online for a knotting technique that speaks to you (some are intricate macrame-like knots, some are very simple). You can place your *sekimori ishi* at the end of a path or in a central garden position as a memorial for a treasured pet. I recently made one in commemoration of my dear cat, who has moved on from our astral plane. Her path continues while mine stops at her stone. She has gone forth alone, I cannot follow.

MANNERS 礼儀

Gratitude and small gestures are part of every day on your Tokyo holiday. A polite bow when saying hello or goodbye. Always giving thanks for food. Taking your shoes off to enter a special space. Having your drinks poured for you, or warm towels presented to you at the table before you eat. Really taking notice of the person you are talking to, remembering their name and the uniqueness of your acquaintance, is very important. Japanese manners are deeply embedded in my experience of Tokyo. I am often greeted with the phrase *hisashiburi*, which basically means 'Long time no see', at a cafe or store I have only visited a handful of times.

DIY I love to add Japanese manners to my daily life. Taking my shoes off before entering a private house shows respect for the owners. You can start this as a tradition with your family or housemates – it also puts an end to stomping and keeps floorboards from being damaged by high heels. Bowing may seem a little out of context outside Tokyo, but you can adopt this lovely tradition within your family or try bowing to your cat (they will always appreciate it). Practising and using Japanese phrases to give thanks before and after your meal is not only good manners but helps you and your family or friends learn some of the language. Before a meal, you can use *itadakimasu*, which means 'I humbly receive'. After a meal, seek out your host and tell them: *Gochisousama-deshita* (which literally means, 'It was a great feast').

MOON VIEWING 月見

My favourite Tokyo season is *aki* (autumn). There are leaves changing colour, chestnut *wagashi* (Japanese sweets), warming bowls of udon, woolly jackets and – if I'm lucky enough to have booked my trip at the right time – moon viewing festivals. Known as Tsukimi, Otsukimi or Jyugoya, festivities honouring the moon have been popular in Japan since the Heian Period (794–1185). Changing each year with the lunar calendar, Tsukimi falls somewhere between late September and early October, with traditions including incense burning and food offerings. Locals gather at festivals drinking sake and eating special foods including *tsukimi dango* (dumplings resembling the full moon), sweet potato and chestnuts. As a cute aside: instead of seeing a man in the moon, the Japanese see an *usagi* (rabbit).

DIY Research Tsukimi dates and plan your festivities in advance. If, like me, you live by the opposite seasonal calendar, you can celebrate in your own autumn or during Japan's festival time. In years gone by the Japanese used this festival to give thanks for the harvest using five or ten symbolic *susuki* (pampas grass) tufts. I love to make ikebana from dried grass next to my moon viewing window and carefully arrange my mochi on a mini platform (as I have seen in Tokyo). Prep your celebrations by giving everything a white, circular theme. Find a great recipe and make your own rabbit-shaped mochi. I like to make a soy milk and sake cocktail and, for the kiddies, a vanilla milkshake propped with whiskers and ears. After sunset, look up to deeply appreciate the beauty and mystery of the full moon.

Sentō (communal baths) can be found all over Japan, and in Tokyo are clustered in the more traditional areas like Asakusa and Ueno. *Sentō* are distinguished by the use of heated tap water and sometimes use some added minerals. These aren't to be confused with *onsen* (hot-spring baths), which rely on natural geothermal and volcanic water. Both are places to revive the senses and recharge (and seeing as some *sentō* have electric whirlpool baths, the latter feels like a very appropriate word). Big cities like Tokyo are also known for their 'super' *sentō*. They include all sorts of amenities, from relaxation rooms, massages and saunas to upscale dining.

DIM First, make sure your bathroom is clean and warm. Have a fluffy towel at the ready and put out fresh post-*sentō* clothes. To fashion your own luxurious face mask, take an old facecloth and cut the edges off with fabric scissors. Hold this against your face and, using a pen, mark where your eyes and nostrils rest. Cut these bits out and soak the facecloth for 30 minutes in 1 teaspoon of honey, 4 tablespoons of rice flour and ⅓ cup of whole milk. Run a bath, adding Epsom salts and essential oils (or use Japanese bath salts). Play forest soundscapes and light some candles. Climb into the bath and apply the face mask, steeping for as long as possible. Remove mask and slowly cleanse, tone and moisturise. Follow your *sentō* with an at-home meditation.

SENTŌ 銭湯

Kanji tree radical and mnemonics

ki

hayashi

mori

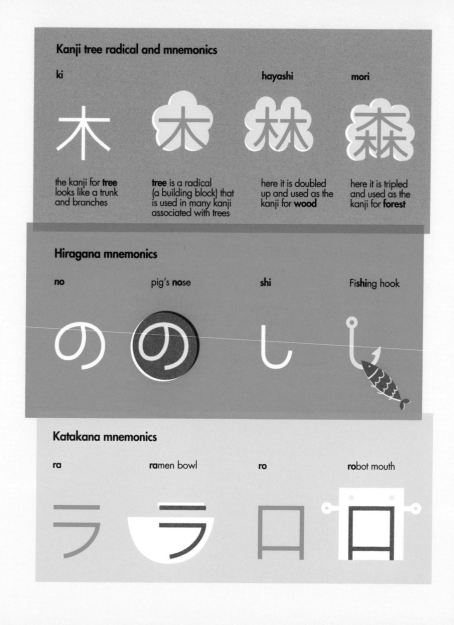

the kanji for **tree** looks like a trunk and branches

tree is a radical (a building block) that is used in many kanji associated with trees

here it is doubled up and used as the kanji for **wood**

here it is tripled and used as the kanji for **forest**

Hiragana mnemonics

no

pig's **no**se

shi

Fi**shi**ng hook

Katakana mnemonics

ra

ramen bowl

ro

robot mouth

LANGUAGE 言語

The Japanese language breaks down into three separate systems of writing symbols: kanji, which originated in China, and Japan's own *hiragana* (ordinary, or simple) and *katakana* (fragmentary). *Hiragana* is used for native Japanese words and *katakana* is used for Western loan words. Both *kana* (sets of written symbols) are syllable groupings. The *kana* are fun to learn through mnemonics and kanji, which can seem quite daunting at first, can be learnt by remembering and memorising sets of radicals (the building blocks of kanji). Basic words for travelling can be retained through online tutorials or podcasts. These might save your life when you can't read the symbol for toilet or don't want squid intestines in your ramen.

DIY Learning a bit of Japanese for a Tokyo trip, even just a few courtesy words, can open a whole new world of possibilities. It's easier than it looks. Start by taking on *hiragana* or *katakana* and go through a YouTube tutorial of all the symbols and how to use them. There are also some great phone apps to help with intonation and mnemonics. You could also pick ten specific words you would like to try to learn. They may be the *kana* for coffee (コーヒー), ramen (ラーメン) or bar (バール) or the kanji for tea, which is made up of both a *hiragana* symbol and a kanji symbol (お茶). Learning the words for hello and thank you shows good manners (and are the bare minimum to learn when visiting any new culture).

Sometimes the manic pace of Tokyo can get to be a bit too much. Near Roppongi, Seishoji Temple holds *zazen* (seated meditation) classes, which I know I can escape to when I'm feeling overwhelmed or in need of focus. First, I wander the beautiful garden, admiring the buildings and grounds, then I participate in the ritual of seated meditation. The greatest benefit to *zazen* is the ability to implement the practice in many – if not all – environments. It's also something you can share with family and friends.

DIY

A home meditation retreat is fun and easy to set up. In a quiet room and wearing comfortable clothing, sit on the floor or a cushion in the lotus position. Cast your eyes downward, place your tongue onto the roof of your mouth and focus on your breath. Breathe in through your nose for a count of five and hold for a count of five before releasing the breath through your mouth. Breathe normally for ten seconds then repeat four or five times. If this doesn't work for you, research other breathing techniques online. It's perfect if you're an insomniac, have a stressful meeting on your calendar or just want to build a mindfulness routine into your everyday.

瞑想

SHICHI
GO
SAN

七五三

On 15 November, Shichi Go San (meaning 'seven five three') is a festival celebrating girls aged three or seven and boys aged five (and sometimes three). A coming-of-age day, its rituals include dressing children in kimono or formal attire and visiting Shinto shrines to pray for their health, happiness and purification. The Meiji Shrine in Harajuku is a perfect place to witness Shichi Go San, and for those travelling with children of the right age, you may consider dressing up your child and joining in the celebrations. Children can be seen carrying a bag of long candy, which symbolises growth, happiness and healthy life.

DIY Do you have a three, five or seven year old? If so, Shichi Go San has family activities that will make your child feel incredibly special. Buy or make a *yukata* (cotton kimono) with an *obi* (sash) in your kid's size. Or dress them in their favourite formal outfit. Make or buy a drawstring bag and add any kind of long candy or food to it (liquorice sticks, Pocky or long lollypops work well). Invite family and friends over to bless your child and try serving food that is long and skinny (like skewered strawberry sticks, bread sticks and dips) or make a Japanese breakfast for all your guests. If you can convince your kid to happily eat grilled fish as part of the traditional breakfast, they're going to have a very blessed life indeed.

OBON お盆

Obon is a Buddhist festival where families gather to revere the dearly departed. Guided by the lunar calendar, it falls somewhere around August each year. Cleaning your ancestor's grave and holding bright lanterns to guide their spirits home (they have re-emerged to visit graves and household shrines) is a mystical and memorable experience. Special foods for the festival include lotus-shaped sweets and there's a ceremonial dance called the Bon Odori. For the last day of Obon, lanterns light up waterways, creating a magical and ethereal sight.

TRADITION

DIY Remembrance of our loved ones is the main message behind Obon. So, visit your departed loved one's grave or the place where their ashes were scattered. Look through photo albums and share stories of your loved one with friends who never met them, or with young family members who never got the chance to know them closely. Make a special meal and share it with family and friends to honour a life well lived. Make or buy lanterns and set them out on your pool or nearby waterway, in what could become part of your family ritual as the anniversary of a passing draws near. Those anniversary milestones are often a time when we check in on friends and family we know to be grieving, but maybe you could make Obon an extra time in the year when you reach out to those experiencing loss.

SUMO 相撲

A sport native to Japan, sumo is steeped in tradition. Although sumo seems simple, the rules are quite complicated. Once you understand them, sumo is mesmerising to watch. I love to walk around Sumida, anywhere close to the Ryōgoku Kokugikan stadium – or 'sumo stables' – and admire off-duty sumo while they shop in their casual *yukata* (cotton kimono) and *geta* (sandals). A martial art, sumo is a male-only sport where giant, scantily clad athletes try to force each other out of a small ring. Shinto rituals, such as purification with salt, take place before each match. Sumo wear *zuna* (braided rope) and *shide* (white paper) around their waist to show rank at special ceremonies.

DIY You'll need to do a crash course in the rules of sumo if you want to enjoy the sport. I like to watch matches on YouTube with English commentary. Tradition and the atmosphere are as important as the match itself. Concentrate on the referee and his spectacular outfits as much as those of the athletes, and make sure you watch a championship ceremony so you can witness the honour bestowed on the winners. There are also guided walks through stables online and interviews with some of the stars. One last takeaway: sumo wear their hair in amazing updos. If you have long hair, try recreating them and perhaps wear them out when you want to channel the power of the sumo.

One of Japan's biggest festivals, Golden Week encompasses four national holidays. One of these is Kodomo no Hi (meaning 'Children's Day'), which is celebrated at the start of May. If you're in the capital at this time, public places will be extra crowded as Tokyoites and visitors from different prefectures come to take a holiday and soak up the atmosphere. Kodomo no Hi uses the symbol of a *koinobori* (a kind of carp-shaped kite or windsock) which are strung up en masse and appear to swim in the sky from high-up places (like Tokyo Tower, for example). Children flit around wearing origami samurai helmets while eating sweet dumplings and sweet rice wrapped in bamboo.

DIY Reserve this day every year to go kite-flying with the big or small children in your life. Pack a picnic or *bento* (lunch box) and ask them to pick the menu. That way they are eating something delicious they know was made just for them. If you buy a white kite for each little one, they can decorate them with fish patterns and shapes using coloured markers. Perhaps one child would fly a manta ray and another a shark or goldfish. Traditionally *koinobori* are red, black or navy blue and have streamers, but it's perfectly fine to follow your own rules. Odds are that the kids will make up their own rules anyway.

KODOMO
NO HI
こどもの日

SHŌGATSU

正月

In Japan, Shōgatsu (meaning 'New Year') is a time for family, celebration and renewal, with distinct customs that are fun to try at home. Held from 1–3 January, celebrations include Hatsumode (the first shrine visit of the year) and feasts called *osechi-ryōri* (New Year festive cuisine). Travelling through Japan at this time of year is a wonderful insight into traditional family customs.

アート＆クラフト

ART
|
&
|
CRAFT

FUROSHIKI

風呂敷

Part of my minimalist luggage regime for every Tokyo trip is packing some *furoshiki* (cloth squares). Always in my daily shoulder bag, I use them to hold my picnic lunch or purchases, or use them often as a headscarf or neckerchief. This special kind of sustainable wrapping came to prominence in Japan in the 700s. *Furoshiki* (square) and *tenugui* (rectangular) cloths have multiple uses but are most commonly the wrapping for presents (and even make great gifts themselves). Forgo plastic bags on your Tokyo trip and carry small belongings with a *furoshiki*. They're versatile, reusable, chic and fuss free.

DIY

I have two basic methods of creating *furoshiki* bag ties with a large piece of square fabric. For the first method, I start by rotating the square so it looks like a diamond and put my item into the middle of the fabric. Then I tie the bottom of the diamond with the left point using double knots and repeat this for the top and right points. I finish by threading the right knots neatly under the left, pulling both up to create a handle. The second *furoshiki* method feels more like wrapping a birthday present. First, pull in and double-knot opposite sides of the diamond. Then, pull in the remaining two sides and carefully tie these over the first double knot. Slide your wrist between the knots to carry.

ORIGAMI 折り紙

The art of folding flat paper into sculptural designs has been popular in Japan since the 17th century. Designers such as Issey Miyake and Junya Watanabe fashioned clothes and accessories using origami as their inspiration, while graphic designers have used intricate folding techniques for brochures, books and other print materials. I love to pleat, flip and fold paper into three-dimensional forms for both creative pursuits and sheer mindfulness. On every trip I've taken to Tokyo, I always need to visit all the top craft shops and bookstores to find the best patterned paper and indulge my love of origami.

DIY There are so many fun and clever origami shapes, folds and wrapping techniques to master so check online for some inspiration that speaks directly to you. Make sure you have a large supply of pretty-patterned or double-sided bicolour papers to flip and fold. Some of my favourite beginner origami shapes to make are hearts, bows, butterflies, frogs, cats and dogs. Medium-difficulty to seriously advanced designs can include intricate flowers, cranes, foxes, dinosaurs and pandas. Beginners can check out @michellemackintosh on Instagram where I have links to my YouTube tutorials on entry-level origami projects.

PRINT

柄

Tokyo designers are celebrated for their bold and layered prints. Trainers, t-shirts, dresses, wrapping paper and journals all get the full Tokyo-style graphic pattern makeover. In a city where design is highly valued, people of all ages and on all budgets adore print. Printed patterns, shapes and colours can clash deliberately to create a strangely balanced hybrid. For *gaijin* (Westerners), a trip to a museum or kimono store can be a revelation. Something that might seem like a contemporary piece from a Japanese designer, like Comme des Garçons, Tsumori Chisato or Minä Perhonen, could actually be a precious antique design.

DIY I have a collection of Japanese biscuit-cutter moulds in various shapes and sizes for baking. I double them up as craft tools to make my own simple potato-printed paper. Firstly, cut a potato in half and press a biscuit cutter into the middle. Then, with a blunt knife, trace around the edges of your biscuit shape. With the biscuit cutter still in place, cut off the top layer (around 1.5cm) of the potato. Discard the edges, remove your biscuit cutter and now the bottom of your potato will have the biscuit shape popping out of the top. Make stamps in a few different designs using different biscuit cutters, dry them off and then hold against an ink pad before pressing them onto paper. I like to make three of the same shape and stamp onto my paper one colour one at a time to make a pattern. Wait for each different colour to dry then overlap the same stamp for a layered look.

Everywhere I look in Tokyo I see patterns. Graphic shapes in food, architecture and nature inform the city. Looking down at a sea of umbrellas from a hotel window, the rows of bamboo at the Nezu Museum, *bento* (lunch boxes) en masse in department stores or the colours and shapes of subway tiles: I play games with myself and try to focus on just red objects or just long shapes. It helps me to see Tokyo from a different perspective and sparks ideas for future creative projects.

DIY Choosing to look closely at my surroundings in detail comes from creative curiosity and an interest in slow-living practices. I like to reserve time to walk my neighbourhood looking for unexpected patterns, documenting my findings on my phone and in my journal. I look for big patterns and small, photographing the same pattern in both micro and macro. I choose details from different kinds of architecture and different textures. I look for circles, stripes and squares. Sometimes I focus on colour, other times on nature. Every time I wander, I notice patterns in unexpected places.

PATTERN 模様

SNAIL MAIL 郵便物

One of my favourite things to do in Tokyo is send home some snail mail. Giving is always more rewarding than receiving when sending something you've written. I make my own envelopes and decorate them with ephemera collected on my travels (of course this means I need to visit all the finest craft stores to buy beautiful washi tape, stickers and rubber stamps). When my snail mail is ready, I head to the post office and select a winner from the incredible array of seasonal stamps. I love sending mail to Japanophile friends and pen pals who appreciate handcrafted news from the capital.

DIY Choose a colour palette and theme, collecting craft materials from local stores and drawing your own designs based on your theme. Make an origami envelope or pretty-up one you already have lying around with some washi tape and stencils. Ask your local post office to show you their limited edition or seasonal stamps. Stuff your envelope with a heartfelt letter, pressed leaves and flowers or a homemade bookmark. Find the best-looking post box nearby (there is a vintage post box near me I always use) and snap a pic of yourself dropping in the letter to send to the recipient if you want to build anticipation. Post away.

ART & CRAFT

From delicate ancient scrolls and Nihonga-style paintings to striking conceptual works by contemporary artists Yoko Ono and Yayoi Kusama, Tokyo houses some of the world's greatest art. In the city, fine art makes its way out of the galleries, enhancing store displays and the fashion within, waiting to be found in gardens and adding mystique to airports and municipal buildings. Many times I've visited Tokyo, the day has turned to night as I've lost track of time in the backstreet bespoke gallery spaces, immersing myself in experiences both rich and varied. I guarantee that Tokyo's art scene will imprint itself on your heart.

DIY Research Japanese art destinations in your own hometown. Many larger galleries will have an Asian art wing, which will likely have a few key Japanese pieces. You may also be surprised to find great examples in private collections that are open to the public on select days throughout the year and at indie galleries that showcase international up-and-coming artists. Have a think about your favourite style of Western art and find out what Japan was creating at the same moment in history. Take a local class in calligraphy, woodblock printmaking or ink painting, or make an online scrapbook of your favourite styles to use as inspiration to fill your sketchbook.

ART 美術

建築 ARCHITECTURE

After the Great Kantō earthquake of 1923 and the Second World War decimated Tokyo, the city picked itself up, dusted itself off and began to rebuild. Pockets of ancient architecture, modernist relics, shrines and temples still remain, sitting curiously beside some of the most interesting contemporary architecture on the world stage. Upmarket Aoyama is wonderful for an afternoon architectural stroll, as is Roppongi's art triangle and many of the city's Christian churches. Phillippe Starck's fondly nicknamed 'Golden Turd' cantilevers out atop the Asahi Building, Kenzo Tange's breathtaking Yoyogi Stadium has a dynamic roof span that scrapes the heavens and Kengo Kuma's Nezu Museum creates a meditative and industrial backdrop for the cultural artefacts within.

DIY Does your city have any Japanese-inspired buildings or spaces? Some quick online research or an email to an expert may uncover some local gems. Research your hometown for interesting buildings, using keywords like mid-century, contemporary, Modernism or Brutalism. Also, research award-winning buildings and open days for personal residences designed by renowned architects. I always travel for architecture, so if you find yourself a couple of hours away from a piece of architectural history, pack a *bento* (lunch box) and get exploring.

HAIKU 俳句

The beloved Japanese short-form poetry called haiku is a three-line verse often working on the pattern of five, seven and five syllables (but not always). These simple and transient poems often focus on the natural world. Devotees and the poetry-curious alike must visit Tokyo's Museum of Haiku Literature and Basho Memorial Hall to soak up the history of this distinct literary form. Some of the greatest haiku writers spent their lives wandering the countryside in search of inspiration. A simple life of quiet reflection enabled these poets to transcribe their exact feelings at a given time using a framework of minimalism, allowing the reader to share that moment with them.

DIY Try composing your own haiku. Read classic examples from Basho, Issa, Shiki and Buson (even Kerouac wrote a book of haiku) and try to absorb the methodology and style. Use sparse phrasing and simple words to frame specific moments in time. Clear your mind of clutter, pare back your thoughts, use only what is needed. The everyday beauty of nature – mountains, streams, flowers and leaves – are haiku's greatest muses. Deceptively simple, your haiku may be an ode to a ladybird, melting snow or the pattern play of nature's shadows on your living room wall.

BORO

ぼろ

Boro (something repaired) is the art of stitching together rags or small pieces of fabric that would otherwise have been discarded. These textiles adorned the uniforms of the working class in the Edo Period, traditionally made with scraps of indigo-dyed natural fabrics stitched together in a way that strikingly clashed patterns and shapes. While the upper classes wore fine silk, the working classes began to repurpose cotton and hemp. The Edo Period created a new urban class who – out of sheer necessity – created new forms of weaving, stitching and dyeing. Today you can find original *boro* at Tokyo flea markets or in Western antique stores for eye-popping prices.

DIY Do you have an old denim jacket or a pair of jeans in need of repair? Have a scout around online for beautiful examples of *boro* then spend an afternoon in vintage stores or in the depths of your wardrobe to find interesting indigo fabrics. Pin or use fusible webbing to attach these indigo scraps to your damaged denim. You'll need an embroidery or *sashiko* (little stabs) needle and thread to stitch together your creation. Look online for great examples of *sashiko* stitching or use a simple running stitch that's loud and proud. Visible mending is an integral part of the *boro* aesthetic. Wear your patchwork design on a night out and get ready for a flurry of compliments and some curious questions.

As a graphic and book designer, it was design that made me fall in love with Tokyo. The branding of the 1964 Tokyo Olympics is a classic masterclass in visual communication. From its bookshops and vintage signage to the 2121 Design Site, Tokyo is any design lover's dream. The city's stationery and art supply stores always inspire me to try new things and experiment with different materials. Ultimately, the thing that strikes me about design in Tokyo is its everydayness – clever functional design is accessible to everyone and can make even nondescript objects feel important and considered.

DIY Take a walk around your neighbourhood or hometown, keeping an eye out for elements of design. Clear your mind and aim to fill your day looking up, down and around at things you'd never usually notice. Book covers in a bookshop, window displays, train signage, the printed fabric on a public seat or the colour of a park bench. Does the combination of your neighbour's bright yellow letterbox against a black-and-white checked patio suit her personality? What reusable bag design is everyone sporting at your local farmer's market? Think about design being in nature, from the leaf you pick up from the ground to the pattern on a bright beetle. Once you've tuned into design you will see how it can bring a heightened sense of whimsy and gratitude to the everyday.

YUKATA AND OBI

浴衣と帯

ART & CRAFT

Yukata (cotton kimono) have beautiful patterns and are tied with an impressive *obi* (sash). They are worn when staying at a *ryokan* (traditional Japanese inn), at *onsen* (hot-spring baths) or to summer festivals and fireworks displays. A wonderful souvenir, I wear an everyday *yukata* at home and have a linen one I wear on special occasions. There is certainly a right and wrong way to wear a *yukata*. A *hadajuban* (white cotton undergarment) is traditionally worn beneath it, which leaves a chic strip of white around the collar.

ACKNOWLEDGEMENTS
謝辞

Thank you to the whole team at Harper By Design and HarperCollins. I'm so blessed to be part of a fledgling imprint whose purpose is to bring beauty to our everyday reading. Thank you to my publisher, the inimitable Mark Campbell, for your insights, support and incredible creativity. It has been a complete joy to work with you from start to finish. Thank you for trusting me and believing in our little book (and for the fluoro pink fifth colour). Thank you to Patrick Boyle for sensitively editing my words, prodding me in the right direction and discovering the beautiful essence of each idea. Thank you to the super-talented Mietta Yans for intuitively knowing how to design with my style in mind and make every page sing. Thank you to my dear-hearted husband Steve Wide for your love, support, inspiration and editorial skills that make it possible for me to be my very best. Thank you to my friend and 'series mate' Alice Oehr for all your generosity and support. Thank you to my dear friend Hiki Komura for teaching me so much about Japanese culture. Last, but not least, thank you to my incredibly supportive family and friends for always being there for me (and to Pizzicato Five for providing the team soundtrack to PYIT).

Harper *by* Design
An imprint of HarperCollins*Publishers*

HarperCollins*Publishers*
Australia • Brazil • Canada • France • Germany • Holland • Hungary
India • Italy • Japan • Mexico • New Zealand • Poland • Spain • Sweden
Switzerland • United Kingdom • United States of America

First published in Australia in 2022
by HarperCollins*Publishers* Australia Pty Limited
Level 13, 201 Elizabeth Street, Sydney NSW 2000
ABN 36 009 913 517
harpercollins.com.au

A catalogue record for this book is available from the National Library of Australia

ISBN 978 1 4607 6234 9

Publisher: Mark Campbell
Publishing Director: Brigitta Doyle
Editor: Patrick Boyle
Japanese proofreaders: Hanna Imai & Hikaru Komura
Designer: Mietta Yans, HarperCollins Design Studio
Author and Illustrator: Michelle Mackintosh
Printed and bound in China by RR Donnelley

8 7 6 5 4 3 2 1   22 23 24 25

Michelle Mackintosh
is an award-winning book
designer, illustrator and author.
She designs and illustrates books
on cooking, gardening, culture and pop
culture for publishers all over the world.
Michelle has written three books on analogue
correspondence and co-written eight books on
Japan, of which many have been translated into
multiple languages. Her love of Japanese design
and culture informs every part of her work and
life: Michelle became obsessed with Japanese
culture in Year Three and for the past 20
years she has spent three months of
the year travelling, drawing and
writing in Japan.